D1581373

'Roger Carswell is not only a fi knows how to inspire others in personal evangelism. His new book, *Evangelistic Living*, is powerful, practical and profoundly motivational. He makes the gospel message clear — the manner of witness effective — the motivation infectious through powerful stories — and in his inimitable style, he leaves us without excuse while rekindling our joy for witness. I loved the book and I think you will too.'

Rebecca Manley Pippert, Author of *Stay Salt*

'Evangelism is not merely an activity that we engage in but it should be a lifestyle that we practice. Having had the joy of knowing Roger over a number of years I can think of no one better to write on this subject. He practises what he preaches and models what he mandates. Read this and turn each day to an adventure of faith as we look for every opportunity to share Christ.'

Michael Ots, Author and University Evangelist

EVANGELISTIC LIVING

Sharing the Gospel Day by Day

ROGER CARSWELL

Scripture taken from the New King James Version®. Copyright © 1982 by Thomas Nelson. Used by permission. All rights reserved.

Copyright © 2020 by Roger Carswell

First published in Great Britain in 2020

The right of Roger Carswell to be identified as the Author of this Work has been asserted by him in accordance with the Copyright, Designs and Patents Act 1988.

British Library Cataloguing in Publication Data
A record for this book is available from the British Library

ISBN: 978-1-913278-43-4

Designed by Jude May
Cover image © Si-Gal | iStock

Printed in Denmark by Nørhaven

10Publishing, a division of 10ofthose.com
Unit C, Tomlinson Road, Leyland, PR25 2DY, England
Email: info@10ofthose.com
Website: www.10ofthose.com

To the zealous foot soldiers who gather annually at the Fellowship of Evangelist Workers' (the FEW) Conference. Your example of faithfully and enthusiastically proclaiming the gospel, often in lonely and challenging situations, spurs me on to boldly and winsomely make Christ known to everyone I meet. To each of you I want to dedicate this book.

Contents

Introduction: Evangelistic Living

Soul-winners are not soul-winners because of what they know, but because of the Person they know, how well they know Him, and how much they long for others to know Him.

Dawson Trotman

The greatest act of service for the Christian each day is to share the gospel with an unconverted person. The greatest use of life's occurrences is to utilise them to proclaim the gospel. Explaining the gospel to another redeems each day, crowning it with the ultimate act of kindness we can show to anyone.

Evangelistic burden comes from belief in what the Bible teaches and walking closely with the Lord. Through the finished work of Jesus on the cross, Christians have found forgiveness and new, eternal life. We have found that God has transformed us so that instead of living for ourselves, we want to live in a way that honours our Saviour and serves those around us. Jesus said, 'Let your light so shine before men, that they may see your good works and glorify your Father in heaven' (Matthew 5:16). We will want to live godly, consistent lives. It is worth remembering, though, that our message is not that we are good, but that we are sinners who have a Saviour who loved us and died for us. Our message is not about our goodness, but about Jesus' grace. I often say to people, 'Christ Jesus came into the world to save sinners, and you and I qualify. If He had come into the world for good people, He would never have found any!'

Throughout history, the church has honoured scholars, and we thank God for them. But according to Daniel 12:3, God honours soul-winners: 'Those who are wise shall shine like the brightness of the firmament, and those who turn many to righteousness like the stars forever and ever.' This is an interesting verse because it occurs just after a description of great tribulation that the saints of God are experiencing, and yet in the midst of such crisis the work of leading people to God is still going on.

I love a particular incident from the days of the prophet Elisha (2 Kings 5:1–10). Living in Damascus was Naaman, the commander of the king's army. He was greatly honoured as a man of valour, but he had leprosy. Serving in his household was a young maid who had been taken captive from her home, her family, her religion. As she lived amongst a people and in a household which was worldly and idolatrous, she would have been pained with home-sickness and isolation. Nevertheless, she kept her sincerity, trust and kindness. Naaman would have known nothing of the law of God. He worshipped at the temple dedicated to the idol Rimmon – the greatest and most beautiful of the many temples in Damascus. How could he ever hear of the true and living God without 'a preacher'? The little maid waited her moment. She had not forgotten the Lord amidst the strangers and strange gods. Neither was she too young or too insignificant to speak up. Verse 3 continues the story: 'Then she said to her mistress, "If only my master were with the prophet who is in Samaria! For he would heal him of his leprosy."' That is the last we read of the little maid. They were simple, unassuming, affectionate words of witness which were to have such a profound effect and lead to Naaman's healing and salvation.

Not every Christian is gifted as an evangelist, but every Christian is a witness. If we are to take seriously the Bible's teaching about heaven and hell, sheer human compassion would leave us longing for everyone to know God's salvation. A burden for lost men and women is an inevitable concern for those in whom the Spirit of God dwells. Each born-again believer has a story to tell of what the Lord has done for them, and desires to do in the hearts of people everywhere. Famously, when Jesus commissioned His disciples before ascending back to His Father in heaven, He said, 'Go therefore and make disciples of all the nations, baptising them in the name of the Father and of the Son and of the Holy Spirit ... Go into all the world and preach the gospel to every creature' (Matthew 28:19 and Mark 16:15). William C. Burns, who was greatly used in the revival in Dundee, Kilsyth and Perth in the days of Robert Murray McCheyne's faithful ministry, had this passion. Once, when he was quite young, he was walking with his parents along Trongate in Glasgow when they suddenly noticed him missing. Quickly, they turned back to find him, not in a sweet or toy shop, but standing in a passage weeping. They enquired what the trouble was, but all he could say through his sobs was, 'Oh, the people! Oh, the people!'

Likewise, Mrs Bowen Thompson was the widow of a missionary doctor who had served the Lord in Antioch and the Crimea. When her husband died of fever, she returned to England. But massacres of Christians were rife throughout the Ottoman Empire, and on reading of women and children who had seen their husbands and fathers brutally murdered, she 'felt specially called to try and alleviate their distress, and make known to them the only balm for a broken heart – the love of Jesus.'[1] Eventually, she was to found the British Syrian Mission. This indefatigable lady would rise at 5 a.m. and follow her daily routine of conducting family prayers; arranging work for the women and girls she was helping; teaching classes; visiting the sick; writing letters; keeping the accounts; making plans; seeing visitors; leading Bible studies; and going 'forth to the haunts of sin' to share Christ. She would often work until one or two in the morning. When her assistant said she could no longer bear the rigours of such days, Mrs Thompson replied, 'How can we enjoy ease while so many are suffering in soul and body?'

Today, every aspect of society is conspiring to silence Christians, with leading media personalities and journalists openly mocking the gospel, ridiculing those who believe it. But this is our Father's world, and nobody has the right

13

to gag Christian witness. The gospel is the very best news anyone can hear. Our message is too precious to be hidden behind church walls, and the needs of men and women are too pressing for us to keep quiet when we have Jesus as our Saviour. It is He who has commanded us to proclaim these good tidings of great joy. We are under marching orders and dare not attempt to be secret disciples. Michael Green said, 'We have something crucial to declare, and must find the best way to do it in an age that is sceptical about God, cynical about truth and unimpressed by ethical demands.'

Throughout the Bible, there is a sense of urgency concerning reaching people with the gospel. Jesus Himself urged us to pray that the Lord of the harvest would send out labourers into the harvest, because the labourers are few (Luke 10:2). This sense of urgency shouts out from invitations recorded throughout the Bible:

- Joshua 24:15 ('… choose for yourselves this day …')
- 1 Kings 18:21 ('How long will you falter between two opinions?')
- Psalm 95:7–8 ('Today if you will hear His voice … Do not harden your hearts …')
- Isaiah 55:1–3 ('Ho! Everyone who thirsts, come to the waters …')

- Ezekiel 33:11 ('Turn, turn from your evil ways. For why should you die …')
- Matthew 11:28–30 ('Come to Me, all you who labour and are heavy laden …')
- Luke 14:17 ('Come, for all things are now ready …')
- 2 Corinthians 5:20 ('… be reconciled to God')
- Hebrews 12:25 ('See that you do not refuse Him who speaks')

If God can urgently plead with people to turn from their sin to receive forgiveness and His eternal life, why wouldn't we echo His heart and cry? In a hundred years from now, all those whom we meet will be in eternity – either in heaven with the Lord, or in hell, lost forever. We never know when will be the last opportunity that someone has to hear and respond to the gospel.

Let me look at the crowd as my Saviour did
'Til my eyes with tears grow dim;
Let me look 'til I pity the wandering sheep
And love them for love of Him.[2]

R.C. Morgan was the editor of a Victorian Christian magazine and well known amongst evangelicals of the late-nineteenth century. He knew sadness in that two of his children died in infancy. His eldest son then drowned whilst swimming in a local river in London. On hearing the news, he made his way quickly to the place where the river was being dredged to try to recover the body. A crowd had gathered, watching the drama. In time they saw the boy's body brought out of the water and laid on the riverbank. Broken-hearted, R.C. Morgan spoke through his tears to the crowd, explaining that this was his son, but adding that the boy was a Christian and so would now be in heaven with his Saviour. He then preached the gospel to them. A remaining son of Morgan's, who wrote his biography, adds that twenty years later R.C. Morgan was in a hosiery shop where he spoke about the Lord to the shopkeeper, who said that he was already a believer. On being questioned about his conversion, the shopkeeper explained that he had been converted the very day he witnessed the body of a boy being brought up from the river and had listened to the boy's father preach the gospel. Praise God for the faithfulness of Morgan in preaching the gospel in season and out of season. But such boldness is not to be confined to the Victorian era only.

Paul Fleming, the founder of New Tribes Mission, said:

When one is abandoned to the Lord Jesus – not to 'cause' or 'programme', but simply to the Lord Himself – then to that individual it matters not whether he be placed in a wheelchair, a hospital bed, a prison cell, in a darkened corner where men never see him, or whether he be set on a pedestal where he may preach Christ before the multitudes! It becomes simply a matter of being a 'bond slave' to the Lord Jesus. Whatever may bring the most glory to Him becomes the consuming passion of his life.

Ephesians 2:10 teaches that we are God's workmanship, created by God for good works. God, who made and saved us, has prepared a journey of service for us. That course may take us through trying, tough times or along very pleasant paths. Our ministry may be over a short period of time (as was the case for John the Baptist) or be one which keeps us serving when actions creak louder than words (as with Caleb)! But we are to live for Jesus and speak of Him in our unique area of service, wherever that may be.

Prof. Donald Wiseman, OBE (Emeritus Professor of Assyriology at the University of London) understood this. When he went to be with the Lord in 2010, I attended his memorial service in London. One of his daughters, in her tribute, reflected not only on his brilliant academic credentials – he spoke eighteen languages – but on his passion to reach everyone with the gospel. She remembered the holidays they had as a family. He would push under the doors of everyone in their hotel an invitation to a Christian service which he would be holding in his room at 11 a.m. on the Sunday morning, and there conduct an evangelistic meeting. Even when dying in hospital, each day he would ask for more gospel tracts as he was giving so many away to doctors, nurses and fellow patients.

These are all inspiring stories that follow in the wake of Bible characters who were characterised by a love for the Lord and so for the lost. When Moses was leading the people of Israel through the wilderness towards the Promised Land, he urged his father-in-law Hobab, a Midianite, to go with them, saying, 'Come with us, and we will treat you well; for the Lord has promised good things to Israel' (Numbers 10:29). Hobab declined the invitation, but Moses persisted, saying how useful Hobab would be to them and promising that 'whatever good the Lord will do to us, the same we will do to you' (Numbers 10:32). Centuries later, the Apostle Paul, who established a pattern of Christian discipleship, once again found himself in prison. He had been unjustly treated, beaten and chained in an inner prison cell in Philippi. But he witnessed to other prisoners, and to the guard whom he led to the Lord. Onesimus, imprisoned with Paul in Rome, was converted through Paul's witness. Julius, Paul's guard who had escorted him to Rome, may even have come to faith. Every situation in life is an opportunity to point and perhaps lead people to Christ.

Jesus spoke a parable about the kingdom of God, which gives insights into the work of evangelism of which it is our privilege to be part. He said:

The kingdom of God is as if a man should scatter seed on the ground, and should sleep by night and rise by day, and the seed should sprout and grow, he himself does not know how. For the earth yields crops by itself: first the blade, then the head, after that the full grain in the head. But when the grain ripens, immediately he puts in the sickle, because the harvest has come.

(Mark 4:26–29)

This parable is the basis from which we may learn four principles about evangelism.

1

We need to ensure that we get the right seed

Samuel Zwemer once addressed a student convention on the needs of the Islamic world, and closed his appeal by walking over to a great map of the Muslim lands. Spreading his arms over it, he said, 'Thou O Christ, art all I need; and Thou, O Christ, art all they need.' He is our urgency.

Leighton Ford[1]

Jesus does not say that the kingdom of God is about giving porridge to the poor, flip-flops to drunken revellers or saving the whale. The gospel is not service to the community, valid as that may be. There are many noble works in which Christians are involved, but Jesus taught that the work of the kingdom of God is getting the word of God into the hearts and minds of people. The idea that we can 'preach the gospel, and if necessary use words' is a million miles from biblical teaching. Whatever is not about God's word is not God's work. Christian work is measured by the place it gives to the word of God and the person of Christ.

Evangelism is very specific. It is proclaiming the gospel to non-Christians who are listening. Jesus, in His Great Commission, spelled out the basic gospel message we are to communicate to those whom we meet: 'Then He said to them, "Thus it is written, and thus it was necessary for the Christ to suffer and to rise from the dead the third day, and that repentance and remission of sins should be preached in His name to all nations beginning at Jerusalem"' (Luke 24:46–47).

The message we are to take to our neighbours (the equivalent of Jerusalem) and all nations is central to the Old and New Testament. It has four basic ingredients.

1. Jesus' sufferings

Jesus came into our world with the express purpose of going to the cross where He would be 'the propitiation for our sins, and not for ours only but also for the whole world' (1 John 2:2). 'For Christ also suffered once for sins, the just for the unjust, that He might bring us to God, being put to death in the flesh but made alive by the Spirit' (1 Peter 3:18). Jesus 'Himself bore our sins in His own body on the tree' (1 Peter 2:24).

The fact that God laid on Jesus the sin of us all is of fundamental importance. The saving power of the cross is central and crucial to our message. What led to Jesus' crucifixion was not the actions of the Jewish authorities or Roman soldiers, but God's love for lost men and women. For this reason Paul wrote to the Corinthians that he was 'determined not to know anything among you except Jesus Christ and Him crucified' (1 Corinthians 2:2).

Jesus died so that we could be forgiven and reconciled to God. It was His love for the lost world that held Him to the cross. The wonder of the cross is not its brutality and blood, but that the Lord of all glory suffered and shed His blood for us. Jesus carrying on Himself our sin is God's greatest work. The holy Son of God not only took the punishment for our sin, but carried on Himself sin that was so abhorrent to Him.

2. Jesus' resurrection

Having paid for our sin, Jesus gave Himself over to death, crying, 'Father, "into Your hands I commit My spirit"'

(Luke 23:46). It was a dead body that they took down from the cross, and the body of Jesus was laid in an unused tomb. It had a huge stone rolled in front of it, and was sealed and guarded. But on the first Easter Sunday morning, Jesus rose again. He had defeated death.

The physical resurrection of Jesus separates Jesus from any other. He, the God-man, conquered the grave. The body that went in to the tomb is the same one that rose again. We proclaim a living, risen Jesus. The triune God was at work in salvation, and in raising Jesus to life. We read that the Father raised Jesus (Acts 5:30; 1 Peter 1:21), that the Holy Spirit raised Him (1 Peter 3:18) and that He raised Himself to life (John 2:19–21).

3. Repentance

John the Baptist, Jesus Himself, Peter and Paul each preached repentance. Every sermon in the Book of Acts contains the twin themes of Jesus' resurrection and repentance.[2] Our message is not simply 'Come to Jesus', but rather that we come with a willingness to turn away from our old life to receive newness of life and forgiveness. We come to Christ as we are, but He doesn't leave us as we are. He makes all things new. There will be a renouncing of all things which could grieve Him, and a relishing of everything which pleases God. As Paul wrote to the Corinthians, 'For you were bought at a price' (1 Corinthians 6:20). That is why we should want to glorify God in our bodies and our spirits.

If repentance is not proclaimed, superficial 'decisions' to profess faith will come easily. Our calling is not decision-making but disciple-making. I have often heard claims of large numbers of 'conversions' at some evangelistic event or other, only to be bitterly disappointed to discover later that none of those who professed faith were seen again. Sometimes claims of several 'conversions' will be made to vindicate the ministry of an evangelistic worker, but this can be dishonest. A lack of integrity like this reveals that one's confidence is in scheming rather than the Lord. There has to be an understanding that true faith in Christ will lead to a change in life. Conversion entails new birth by the Holy Spirit of God, not just an emotional response. Frankly, if a person is not different from how he or she used to be, then 2 Corinthians 5:17 teaches us that the person is not a Christian.

Jesus did not mask the cost to following Him, even if it appeared that He allowed potential followers to slip through His fingers (as seems to be the case of the people we read of in Luke 9:57–62). In Patricia St John's autobiography, *In Her Words*, she recounts the story of a young woman who trusted Christ in Morocco. To leave her Muslim sub-culture was never going to be easy, but the cost came home when she gave birth to her first child. The custom at such a time is that the mother, sisters or family would be around to help, but this woman was left alone because of her Christian faith. With deep feeling she said to Patricia St John, 'But you never told me ...' It is costly to swim against the tide in our secular country, and we must make this clear to those professing faith. Though the Lord will always be with us, to stand up and speak out for Him is tough. Yet I, for one, would never trade the joy of knowing the Lord for all the friends or accolades the world has to offer. Jesus has never been a disappointment, and to speak about Him always gives me great pleasure.

4. Forgiveness

The Holy Spirit convicts people of sin, and only God can forgive the very transgressions which are primarily against Him. Sin is serious. It is the absolute betrayal of all for which we were created. There are so many promises in the Bible which speak of forgiveness:

'Come now, and let us reason together,'
Says the LORD,
'Though your sins are like scarlet,
They shall be as white as snow;
Though they are red like crimson,
They shall be as wool.'

(Isaiah 1:18)

For as the heavens are high above the earth,
So great is His mercy toward those who fear Him;
As far as the east is from the west,
So far has He removed our transgressions from us.
(Psalm 103:11–12)

I have blotted out, like a thick cloud, your transgressions,
And like a cloud, your sins.
Return to Me, for I have redeemed you.

(Isaiah 44:22)

For You have cast all my sins behind Your back.'
(Isaiah 38:17)

You will cast all our sins
Into the depths of the sea.

(Micah 7:19)

Then Peter said to them, 'Repent, and let every one of you be baptised in the name of Jesus Christ for the remission of sins; and you shall receive the gift of the Holy Spirit. For the promise is to you and to your children, and to all who are afar off, as many as the Lord our God will call.'

(Acts 2:38–39)

If we confess our sins, He is faithful and just to forgive us our sins and to cleanse us from all unrighteousness.

(1 John 1:9)

The offer of forgiveness from God is beyond anything we could imagine for God is holy and just, but altogether loving. He repeatedly promises, 'For I will forgive their iniquity, and their sin I will remember no more' (Jeremiah 31:34; cf. Hebrews 8:12).

Forgiveness is not earned or bought, but received as a gift. Heaven is not a reward for good deeds, but a gift purchased by Jesus and offered by Him, and it is to be received by faith. To reject Jesus is to reject forgiveness and eternal life. 'For God did not send His Son into the world to condemn the world, but that the world through Him might be saved' (John 3:17).

The sufferings of Jesus, His resurrection, repentance and

forgiveness of sins are the basic ingredients of the gospel. A message without these fundamentals is not the gospel. I remember once asking a friend about the evangelist who had just spoken at a large university Christian Union carol service. He replied that about 1,000 students had been present, but of the speaker he just commented, 'Great communicator; no gospel, but great communicator!' It is the seed of the gospel which we must be sowing if we desire to see the kingdom of God extending and people truly converted.

There is a great urgency for men and women to hear the gospel, and to repent and believe. Every person has an eternal destiny. In 100 years from now, everyone alive today will be in eternity. Heaven could not be more wonderful – Christians will be with Jesus eternally. But hell is desperately sad. To be lost forever without Christ and without hope is too bad for words to describe or the mind to imagine. Practically, that means that our families, friends, colleagues and those with whom we rub shoulders day by day urgently need to get right with God. I love the words of the Wycliffe Bible translators' chorus, 'Every person in every nation, in each succeeding generation, has the right to hear the news that Christ can save'. The truth of that challenges us to prioritise gospel work.

Amy Carmichael (1867–1951) was born in Millisle, Northern Ireland, and converted to Christ whilst boarding at Harrogate Ladies' College. She worked as a missionary in Japan, Ceylon and then, for fifty-five years, Southern India. Her tales of missionary work, as well as her poems and prose, were greatly loved in the first half of the twentieth century. She wrote:

O for a passionate passion for souls,
      O for a pity that yearns!
O for the love that loves unto death,
      O for the fire that burns!
O for the pure prayer-power that prevails,
      That pours itself out for the lost!
Victorious prayer in the Conqueror's Name
      O for a Pentecost!

Many of God's people are characterised by this inner compulsion to make known what God has revealed. David said, 'The Lord gave the word; great was the company of those who proclaimed it' (Psalm 68:11). Amos declared, 'The Lord GOD has spoken! Who can but prophesy?' (Amos 3:8). Jeremiah wrote, 'But His word was in my heart like a burning fire shut up in my bones; I was weary of holding it back, and I could not' (Jeremiah 20:9). The early disciples, threatened by the establishment figures of the day, didn't fear their threats but instead preached the word to them, stating, 'For we cannot but speak the things which we have seen and heard' (Acts 4:20). I heard of this same craving from my hostess when I was speaking at an evangelistic fiftieth birthday party on the Isle of Man. When she was driving me to the airport, she recalled her last flight. Her plane had been delayed by five hours. She thought through her situation: she was in a foreign country; she could do whatever she wanted. Then she said to herself, 'I know what I would like to do – talk to people about Jesus!' She spent the whole time sitting next to people who were travelling and spoke to them about the Lord.

The Apostle Paul wrote, '... I also please all men in all things, not seeking my own profit, but the profit of many, that they may be saved. Imitate me, just as I imitate Christ' (1 Corinthians 10:33 – 11:1). He exemplified this by his life: when he visited a strange town, he cast out demons; when he took up tent-making beside an unbelieving Jew and his wife, he led them to Christ; when he was thrown in prison, he brought the prison guard and his family to faith; when he stood before a judge, he almost persuaded him to be a Christian; and when he was a prisoner in a hired house, he spoke to all who came to him about the gospel. Always and everywhere, he made himself a soul-winner.

Jesus' Great Commission is not to talk theology over a latte; it is not simply to regularly attend every possible meeting and conference. The Great Commission is to go into all the world and preach the gospel to every creature. It is too easy for us as Christians to neglect reaching the lost by being distracted by lesser things.

Once a little-known photographer, Kevin Carter, was in Sudan during the famine of 1993. He was snapping shots of dying children when he heard a high-pitched whimpering in a bush. Investigating, he saw a child with his dark eyes sunken back in his head. His little belly was bloated. Flies were swarming around his head. The child was trying his best to crawl to a feeding centre just a short distance away. Whilst Carter was standing there, a vulture alighted close to the child. The photographer backed up and captured the child, the feeding centre and the vulture all in one picture.

The New York Times bought the picture and ran it on their front page. It also made the cover of *Time* magazine. Kevin had taken a picture which moved millions. Fourteen months later, he received the Pulitzer Prize for photography. Two months later, he drove to his boyhood town, parked his car where he used to play as a child and attached a hose to the exhaust pipe. He ran it in through the side window, left the engine at idle and lay down in the seat. In a few minutes he was dead.

This young photographer had a brilliant career ahead of him. Why would he do something so destructive, so final?

He had received hundreds of letters every day after the photograph was first published. They praised his picture, but almost each one asked the same question: 'What happened to the child?' He had no answer. It had taken twenty minutes to set up the equipment; he took his photograph; then he took down the equipment and left. The fact he had done nothing for the child drove him to the brink. In the depths of regret and guilt, he took his own life.

We cannot just moan or despair about the situation of our world and how lost men and women are. We have to respond, and do so in obedience to the Great Commission.

We are not called to be like the Old Testament prophets, whom the Lord instructed to denounce the sins of the nation. We have been given a different message to proclaim: the good news of Jesus. Around us there are many signs of the people of our nation turning their back on God. Our response is to present the truth that God commands all people to repent whilst at the same time, as John Wesley often said, 'Give them Christ'.

Repeatedly in the Book of Acts, we find the Apostle Paul giving his testimony of conversion (see Acts 22:3ff and 26:12ff). That is because sharing how we came to faith is not only a unique story, but interesting. Everybody loves a good human interest story, so it can be a very easy way in to speak of Christ. When we do so, we will want to explain what we were like before our conversion, and then how we heard the gospel and our response to it. We should share too the difference Jesus has made to our life. In retelling our testimony, we also need to focus on the four vital ingredients of the gospel. We must include an explanation of the atoning death of Jesus, His resurrection, and how we repented and received forgiveness. Maybe you might consider writing your testimony and producing it as a tract. I have written a 900-word gospel leaflet called 'This is my story', which is my testimony or, as I call it, 'My autobiography'! I find it useful to pass on to certain friends.

Romans 1:16 begins, 'For I am not ashamed of the gospel of Christ, for it is the power of God to salvation for everyone who believes ...' From this we learn that the gospel, when proclaimed, is not a philosophy to be discussed or an idea to be debated, but a power to be unleashed. The Holy Spirit loves to honour the Son; when the cross is proclaimed, He speaks pointing the listener to Jesus. The love Jesus demonstrated at Calvary is compelling. As Jesus Himself foretold, His being lifted up on the cross draws people to Himself (John 12:32). God honours those who honour Christ and His cross.

Bishop J.C. Ryle wrote:

Let others hold for the terrors of hell and the joys of heaven … Give me the cross of Christ. This is the only lever, which has ever turned the world upside down and made people forsake their sins. And if this will not, nothing will. A man … will do little or no good among his hearers unless he knows something of the cross. Never was there a person who did much for the conversion of souls who did not dwell on Christ crucified.

In explaining the gospel, we will focus on the cross of Jesus, but it is He who told would-be followers that they would have to take up their cross and follow Him. Dr Samuel Zwemer, a pioneer missionary to Muslims, said, 'Jesus Christ never hid His scars to win a disciple'. Nor should we.

If we are now clear as to the exact seed we must sow, we then need to work prayerfully at getting the gospel seed sown into the ground. We will see how this can be done next.

2

We need to sow and scatter the seed

The Lord gave the word; great was the company of the preachers.

George Frideric Handel[1]

The greatest act of kindness is to tell someone the good news of Jesus; the greatest act of tyranny is to know the gospel and not share it.

Therefore, if we are to be dedicated in the task of making Jesus known, there has to be an attitude of intentionality. I begin my day having a quiet time where I spend precious minutes with the Lord. It is a dogged, daily, delightful discipline to meet with God. I read a portion of the Bible and pray as I commune with God and commit myself afresh to Him. I also pray that God would give me opportunities to speak about Him to those whom I meet.

C.H. Spurgeon advocated such personal evangelism with these words: 'If you had 100 empty bottles before you, and threw a pail of water over them, some would get a little in them but most would fall outside. If you wish to fill the bottles, the best way is to take each bottle separately and put a vessel full of water to the bottle's mouth.' That is the essence of personal work. Evangelist D.L. Moody said the same: 'The way to reach the masses is to reach them one by one.'

Outside of Salvation Army circles, the name of Samuel Logan Brengle is largely forgotten. He had turned his back on being minister of one of the USA's largest and most affluent churches to work with the Salvation Army, reaching out to people in the most deprived areas. Eventually, he became a Commissioner with them, and one of their most loved and influential leaders. In Clarence Hall's biography of him we read:

It often happened that many of the souls he won received their blessing in the most unlikely place. Sitting in a dentist's chair, he would tackle the dentist while the dentist tackled his teeth. Having conversation with a newspaper reporter, he would take over the questioning, and the interviewed would interview the interviewer. Recuperating in a convalescent home, he became disturbed about the spiritual condition of those who were treating him, and the doctored began to doctor the doctors. He seldom entered a lift without leaving the operator a cryptic saying to think over; thus:

BRENGLE: 'Your life is full of ups and downs, isn't it?'
LIFT OPERATOR: 'It is that, sir,' smiling.
BRENGLE: 'Well, be sure that your last trip is up, won't you?'[2]

As a teenager, I read a biography of the great nineteenth-century evangelist, D.L. Moody, who ensured that each day he spoke with an unconverted person about Christ. As it happened, I found that each of the next three days, I too shared the gospel with a non-Christian. I remember then praying to the Lord that with His help I would never let a day go by without speaking to someone about Jesus. I have missed some days, but that discipline has been such a blessing to me. It has helped me to keep close to the Lord, and go through each day looking for opportunities to speak.

We read of Jesus that He entered Capernaum and could not do many mighty works there because of their unbelief

(Matthew 13:58). What does that mean? Surely unbelief did not paralyse the power of Christ. Our unbelief is not greater than His omnipotence. Rather, I think it means that because of their unbelief, those who needed Jesus were not brought to Him and so were not healed by Him. Elsewhere, we see that when people had knowledge of Christ, they brought people to Him and He healed them. The failure of Capernaum was that needy people were not brought to the feet of Jesus.

Personal witness begins by simply talking to people. As long as we don't appear odd or imposing, most people are happy to chatter about anything: the weather, what's going on in the area or in the news, and always about themselves. I then try to introduce Jesus into the conversation. It is not difficult to do. The day before writing this, I was checking into a Travelodge for the night. The receptionist just quipped, 'It's nice to serve a smiley person!' I replied, 'When I was a teenager, I became a Christian by putting my trust in Jesus as my Saviour, and one of the things He has done is put a smile on my face!' She then began to talk about reading a Bible story book to her daughter each night, and so we started chatting.

Conversation may be with the person standing beside us in the bus queue, or at a supermarket checkout, or with someone sitting next to us on a train or tube. As I chatter, I see where the conversation leads. I might say something like, 'It's interesting you say that, because I was in church the other Sunday when our minister said something about that ...' Or I might comment, 'It's interesting you say that because I was reading in my Bible the other day that Jesus said ...' Or I might simply explain that 'I am a Christian and I have found that ...' Sometimes, I just ask if the person ever goes to church. I was once sitting on a bench next to a canal in Amsterdam, my bicycle propped next to me. Looking the other side of a bridge across the canal, I noticed large painted words in Dutch on a building. So I asked the person sitting near me what the words meant. He replied, 'It means "God is my bridge".' We began to talk! The conversation was so good that when he eventually moved on, I decided to stay and ask those who came to sit on the bench the same question. I spent a few hours witnessing to people there using the same approach!

I have a friend who is not a natural 'talker', but he is a good artist. He will sit on a bench and in a few moments draw a portrait sketch of someone sitting near him. He will then show it, asking if they would like the picture. They always respond with 'Yes please!' Finally, he asks their name and under the sketch writes, 'Jesus loves you

…!' adding their name! Now that is using a God-given talent for the Lord.

The value of using tracts

Over a century ago, the founder of the Hawes Creamery (famous for Wensleydale Cheese), then a teenager, noticed a piece of paper on the street in Hawes. Inquisitively, he picked it up, read it and was converted to Christ. The discarded tract had done its work.

James Hudson Taylor, who became a pioneer missionary to China, was so bored with his life in Barnsley he took a tract to his family's outhouse, intending simply to read the opening story. But reading on, he came to the words 'the finished work of Christ'. He trusted Jesus as his Lord and Saviour … and the rest is history.

It was a pamphlet, written by Martin Luther, falling into the hands of John Bunyan which helped him to Christ. He became the author of *Pilgrim's Progress*.

There are many other stories like this, but are tracts valuable today? I would answer a thousand times, 'Yes!' The vast majority of people in the United Kingdom have never heard a clear explanation of the gospel message. They pass through life and into eternity with a religion that has been shaped only by their home, school assemblies and the media. Their attitude to Jesus, if they believe in Him, is to benevolently respect Him as a good teacher from history, but they think He has little relevance to them individually. They must hear the news that only He can save, and they urgently need to repent and believe.

Of course, the ideal would be for each person to hear the gospel either in church, a mission or from a Christian, but there are millions of people to reach. That is where tracts are so valuable. A good tract (or Christian leaflet, as I prefer to call it), which is attractively designed and a faithful gospel explanation, can be a powerful proclaimer of the gospel. It never gets tongue-tied; it is not cowardly or compromising in its presentation; it can quote and explain Scripture; and it leads its reader to a prayer of true repentance and faith. It does not answer back, or become irritated when ignored. It doesn't wait until Sunday to present the good news. It can be read in the bustle of a busy life or in quietness, at any time of the day or night. Tracts, like dynamic evangelists, have a personality and power of their own. They are like missionaries, going into all situations to testify of Jesus.

Long ago, God commanded His people to care for the materially poor and debtors, but it seems to me that the words equally apply to us with regard to the spiritually poor debtors: 'If there is among you a poor man of your brethren … You shall surely give to him … for this thing the LORD your God will bless you … therefore I command you, saying, "You shall open your hand wide to your brother, to your poor and your needy, in your land"' (Deuteronomy 15:7, 10–11).

I have disciplines in my life that I seek to follow. A key one is to never go anywhere without a pocket Bible and a selection of gospel tracts on different themes. I carry them in a wallet that I regard as a great evangelistic tool.[3] I then use them, and 'lose' them!

I use them as the key to open the door of conversation. If there is no queue behind me, I will offer them to the attendant at the garage, or the supermarket checkout, or the bank or newsagent. I will say, 'Before I go, may I give you a small Christian leaflet. It's nothing odd, but simply explains how Jesus came into the world for people like you and me.' Quickly judging their reaction, I see if the conversation will lead to speaking more of Jesus. I pray each day that I will be able to turn inconsequential chatter into significant conversations about Jesus. I aim to be winsome, genuine, chirpy and warm; I don't want people to be put off the gospel because I come across as odd. If they don't want to talk, I leave the subject and simply try to remain friends.

Other times, I will use a tract to close the door of conversation. After having had the opportunity to witness, I leave the person with a suitable leaflet, explaining, 'It goes over some of the things we have just chatted about.' I try to stress that this is 'the ordinary Christian message, not some strange new religion'.

I like to 'lose' tracts as well. I put them in all my correspondence when paying bills, returning forms or simply sending a letter. I send tracts in pre-paid envelopes that are often enclosed in the advertising letters I receive. I 'lose' them on the seat of a bus, train or plane on which I may have travelled. Sometimes, I leave them in telephone kiosks, library books or places where I know they will be found. Then I pray that the Lord will use them.

If I travel overseas, I always obtain some tracts or Gospels in the native language. I then pass them on to waiters, hoteliers and other people I encounter.

For me, tracts are one of the most helpful tools to keep me diligent in scattering gospel seed each and every day. They are not expensive and are easy to pass on. I am encouraged in this by Bible truths like these: 'Cast your bread upon the waters, for you will find it after many days' (Ecclesiastes 11:1); 'Those who sow in tears shall reap in joy. He who continually goes forth weeping, bearing seed for sowing, shall doubtless come again with rejoicing, bringing his sheaves with him' (Psalm 126:5–6).

Some years ago, I had the privilege of leading a Vietnamese PhD student at Bath University to Christ. His conversion began with a prayerfully given tract. He had recently arrived in the country, but felt lonely. One Saturday afternoon, whilst in the town centre, a very elderly lady gave him a tract and an invitation to her Gospel Hall. (As it happens, this lady was the daughter of the famous Bible teacher W.E. Vine.) He regularly attended for several weeks. It was my privilege to be with him at his conversion.

In Musselburgh, I interviewed a man in his forties who had been converted through reading tracts that had been sent in pre-paid envelopes to the Royal Mail in Edinburgh where he worked. He had not had any other contact with the gospel. Another man I knew had come to Christ as a railway carriage cleaner. Working through the night, he saw and read a tract, and there and then prayed to trust the Lord.

> *There's a work for Jesus,*
> *ready at your hand;*
> *'Tis a task the Master*
> *just for you has planned.*[4]

46

Maybe that work for you is to seek to regularly give away gospel leaflets, some of which may lead to significant conversations that count for eternity. I have found that one of the greatest sources of joy each day is to give away a tract!

Good questions and conversation
Personal evangelism is hard work until the person asks a question. I regard any question, even if it is cynical, as an invitation to continue talking. For example, my ear drum may hear someone remarking, 'You don't believe that, do you?' but my brain hears something different: 'Feel free to carry on talking, because I am willing to chat!'

Fear of failure should not prevent us from witnessing. We know that many, perhaps most, will not respond to the gospel as we wish, but the greatest failing is to be disobedient to the Great Commission. George Whitefield and a fellow preacher were staying at an inn. Their attempts to sleep were disturbed by some drunken soldiers in the adjoining room, whose blasphemies and obscene songs disturbed them. Whitefield eventually exclaimed, 'I must go and speak to them, and rebuke them for their language.' The other evangelist asked, 'What is the use? It will only make them worse.' Nevertheless, Whitefield rose from his bed and went to speak faithfully to the godless crowd, only to be mocked by them. As he returned to his room, the oaths and songs were sung more loudly. 'What have you gained by that?' his friend enquired. 'A peaceful conscience,' came the reply!

It is good to be asked questions, but in personal work it is better to ask questions. In fact, in a society where people are basically unaware of spiritual issues, it is vital to get people thinking by stirring their minds to consider where they are with God. Reading through the Gospels, we see that Jesus frequently asked questions.

Francis Schaeffer, who was so fruitful in his ministry amongst people whose thinking had been scarred, said that if he had an hour with someone, he would listen for fifty-five minutes and then speak. I might balance things a little differently, but he was making an important point. We can be so keen to share that we are not taking into account where the people are at. Listen, learn and then seek to introduce them to the gospel.

1 Peter 4:4 reminds us how the non-Christian sees us: 'they think it strange that you do not run with them'! We once lived as they do: 'we walked in lewdness, lusts, drunkenness, revelries, drinking parties, and abominable idolatries' (verse 3), but now our Lord Jesus has transformed

us and we are not doing the same things. We need patience and love to reach out to people who spiritually are blind but so urgently need the gospel.

Of course, there is a different approach in witnessing to those whom we know well, compared to those whom we will perhaps never see again. For those whom I see regularly, I will pray for the right moment to speak. However, I try to take any gospel opportunities to speak to people I just happen to meet in the course of life. It is good to make it known as soon as possible that we are Christians, but we may have to wait for the right moment to speak. Ideally, it is best if we have the opportunity to speak one-to-one. If you can meet and chat individually, there will more likely be a greater willingness to speak, whereas there can be a desire to keep up appearances if people are in a group. Indifference and antagonism are the politically correct reactions to the gospel today, and people may not want to break rank from their peer group.

It is so encouraging to engage in a conversation which is clearly 'a divine appointment'. God has been speaking to the person – maybe someone else has been praying for them – and then we meet with them and have the opportunity to lead them nearer the Lord. But the Lord wants the gospel to go to 'every creature' – people need the Lord, whether or not they realise it. So whether it appears that the person is interested in the gospel or not, it is a privilege, responsibility and joy to speak with them about Jesus. I want to meet lost people and tell them the way of salvation. I sometimes pray that I will be able to bring people one step nearer to Jesus. Some of those are a million miles away, but others are just one step away.

Being creative

There are many other ways in which the good news about Jesus can be shared. Beautiful Christian greeting cards and postcards are available, and it is so easy to simply write a note on them which passes on some gospel truth. There are many lonely people who would love to receive a letter or card that points them to Jesus. A letter to a grandchild may be kept for years as a precious possession, and repeatedly read for many years to come.

In the days of C.H. Spurgeon, a church minister had to stand down from preaching through illness. Looking for a new means of evangelism, he obtained a list of the lonely lighthouse keepers around our coasts, and began writing and sending them printed copies of Spurgeon's sermons. He had some translated into other languages so he could send them to lighthouse keepers overseas. He became the lighthouse keepers' evangelist, though he never met any of them.

William Guthrie was born in 1620 and was heir to his father's estate in Angus, Scotland, but he was converted when he was young. He then set his heart on gospel ministry. An evangelist at heart, he was never satisfied with the masses that came to his church, but concerned for those who never came to church. His ingenuity and creativity led him to many unique opportunities. G.N.M. Collins recalls in his biography how Guthrie:

… in the guise of a traveller would call at one of these godless homes, and in course of conversation, would mention the strange new minister who had come to the parish and make them so curious about him that a visit to the Church followed and a church-going habit was formed. Or he would arrive at a house late at night asking for lodging, and then startle his hosts by proposing family worship before they retired for the night. Sometimes he would equip himself with fishing tackle, for he was an expert angler, and ingratiate himself with people who fished the streams of Ayrshire, some of whom found ere the day was done that they were firmly hooked by the gospel.[5]

Guthrie even bribed away a poacher from his illegal activities by paying him more if he would come to church. The man was soon brought to the Lord, and attended church without being paid to do so!

Door-to-door evangelism

In recent days, I have found that door-to-door evangelism is proving to be more effective than a few years ago when the Jehovah's Witnesses had scuppered the 'open door' of opportunity. To visit on behalf of a local church, but with the intention of speaking not only about the church but about Jesus, can be very heart-warming. I was greatly encouraged in this when reading the autobiography of Richard Hobson. For thirty-three years, in the late-nineteenth century, he was the vicar of a newly formed parish in a very challenging area of Liverpool. Six people were in his congregation when he arrived. There were 3,000 when he left. He believed that 'he that winneth souls is wise' and daily he went looking for them wherever he could. He wrote this about door-to-door work:

I still systematically visited from house to house, attaching great value to that form of ministration, which I took great value to make something more than a simple how-do-you-

do call. My visits were of a teaching character, in the sense of always utilising any opportunity – and one was almost sure to occur – for dropping appropriate words, which, like good seed, might germinate, and bring forth fruit; just following the example of Paul, who taught from house to house, as well as in public.

There is visiting, and visiting. It needs a prayerful heart, and a discerning mind, always to say the right word, at the right time, in the right way. Though it is not always possible to read the word, or to have prayer, in the homes of the poor, it is always possible at least to leave on the peoples' minds the impression that one is a heaven-sent messenger, seeking their good in every way. ... A house-going parson makes a church-going people.[6]

I believe we need to reset our thinking about door-to-door work. Our authority is the Bible. We are not promoting our own opinions, nor trying to put the world straight. We are passing on God's word. I always carry with me a pocket Bible, and love to open it and point out Bible verses, even to unbelievers. Opening and reading the Bible is like opening the mouth of God and letting Him speak. At times I carry just a small New Testament, though I remember Alec Motyer gently rebuking me by saying I was carrying a sword without a handle! I love to quote a verse with the words, 'The Bible says …' Or, if I am not actually quoting, I state, 'The Bible teaches …' I thank God for the work of the Gideons, and when I can, I encourage people to ask them for one of their Gospels to read.

Using the Bible

I remember being in a Vitamin Store in the USA, where I got into conversation with the lady behind the counter. I'm not sure how we moved on to talking about the Lord, but after a few moments, she told me that she was a pagan. I asked her what sort of pagan, to which she added that she was a tree-hugger, explaining that this was because she 'didn't believe all the nonsense in the Bible'. When I asked her to explain, she said, 'Well, things like the world being flat.' We talked more, before eventually I showed her Isaiah 40:21–22. She was really stunned. I continued, 'May I suggest that whoever told you that the Bible teaches that the world is flat probably told you other things about the Bible which are not true.' She agreed, and later agreed to take a Gideon New Testament and read it. It was the Bible that broke through the barrier she had built against God.

One of my good friends was a coal miner. He worked at the coalface in Yorkshire for twenty-seven years. Brought up in a typical working-class, non-Christian home, he was converted in his late teens. He was first 'spoken' to when reading an advert on the back of a Leeds City Council bus ticket. It said, 'For God so loved the world, that He gave His only begotten Son...' (John 3:16). The second part of the famous verse would have been printed on the next ticket, which he didn't have! But this was enough to make him find the Bible he was given when he was at school. He began to read, then to go to a church, where he was converted. I could tell a similar story about a man who was 'arrested' by God through reading a Bible text on a placard outside a church. God had spoken to him, and sometime after he was converted. As the seed of the word of God is sown and scattered, we can expect growth and fruit – as we will see in the next chapter.

There is not only great spiritual ignorance amongst people today, but they have negative views about the message they have never heard and towards the people who believe it. Courses such as Christianity Explored and Stranger on the Road to Emmaus have proved so helpful in introducing people to the message of the Bible. Currently, the Lord is using one-to-one Bible study to do this. *The Word One to One* is devised so that Christians can take someone who knows nothing about Christian things through John's Gospel. Reading *Dare and Persevere*, I found that women were using a similar method of evangelism in the mid-nineteenth century in the Middle East:

> *They visit several families and collect some neighbours, and while one reads a chapter, the others ask questions. This is the only way in which we can have any profitable conversation on the Bible. The women are so excessively ignorant [about the Bible] that they know not how to ask or to answer a question, and in this way they get interested and join in the conversation.*[7]

> *Oh! For a heart that is burdened!*
> *Infused with a passion to pray;*
> *Oh! For a stirring within me;*
> *Oh! For His power every day.*
> *Oh! For a heart like my Saviour,*
> *Who, being in agony, prayed.*
> *Such caring for others, Lord, give me;*
> *On my heart let burdens be laid.*
> *My Father, I long for this passion,*
> *To pour myself out for the lost –*
> *To lay down my life to save others –*
> *To pray, whatever the cost.*

Lord, teach me, Oh teach me this secret,
I'm hungry this lesson to learn,
This passionate passion for others,
For this, blessed Jesus, I yearn.
Father, this lesson I long for, from Thee –
Oh, let Thy Spirit reveal this to me.

Mary Warburton Booth

3

We need to wait and water the seed

In our desire to win souls to Christ, we sometimes forget that these souls have bodies, and that often these lives are bruised. Sometimes they have been bruised by other witnesses! It never hurts to take time to pour in the oil and wine. The way to a sinner's heart is often through his bruises.

Warren W. Wiersbe[1]

Patience does not come naturally in evangelism. We want to be effective; we look for conversions and growth. But though we are responsible for sowing the seed, growth and fruitfulness is God's work. The Bible teaches both that we are co-labourers with God and that He works with us (Mark 16:20 and 2 Corinthians 6:1). Amazingly, God graciously makes us partners in reaching the lost world, but how eternal, spiritual work is done is beyond our understanding and our control. This calls us away from despondency to humility and action.

We long for people to be converted the first time they hear the gospel, but often it is a process that takes time, and during which we don't really know what is happening spiritually. I taught in a boys' secondary school in West Yorkshire for eight years. After I had been there for two terms, a maths teacher started. He was a very effective teacher, but an atheist. He and his wife became good friends with my wife and me. We would meet for meals and chat, and went together to evangelistic meetings, but he remained an atheist. When I moved to teach in another school, we kept in touch. Eventually, I left teaching to work as a full-time evangelist, but we still occasionally met up.

Having known each other for twenty-seven years, we were enjoying an evening together when my wife invited them to a Christianity Explored course which was beginning at our church. He asked if he could bring his Scottish terrier along! Sure enough, they came with their dog. It took a couple of weeks before they engaged in the course, but by the end they had become friends with everyone else there. He asked me for a Bible, which he read through, but was still unconvinced. He then read through a 1,600-page Bible commentary. Eventually, through the witness of those on the course, he came to trust Christ as his Lord and Saviour. When he was baptised, we gave him a *Systematic Theology*. Later, he phoned to say that he and his wife were loving it – reading a chapter each night before going to sleep. But it took nearly twenty-eight years of praying, befriending and witnessing. Though we can't give that much time to everyone, there are some people whom the Lord lays on our heart. We must witness faithfully to them whilst waiting for the Lord to convict them of their sin and speak to their hearts.

The Bible character Ezekiel is helpful here. Whilst he was with other exiles by the River Chebar in Babylon, he was called to be a prophet. God showed him some amazing truths through visions (Ezekiel 1:1). In Ezekiel 37, God took him to a valley of bones. Before, behind and beside him were dead, dry, decaying bones. God asked Ezekiel, 'Son of man, can these bones live?' (verse 3). How could Ezekiel reply? He could hardly say 'no' because it was the omnipotent God who was asking the question, but it didn't really seem possible that the bones would live. Ezekiel, a true diplomat, replied, 'O LORD GOD, You know!' God then spoke, 'Prophesy to these bones, and say to them, "O dry bones, hear the word of the LORD ...'" (verse 4). As Ezekiel preached, the bones came together so that there were skeletons surrounding him. He continued to preach. The skeletons became covered with tendons and skin. Now there was a mighty army of corpses. God continued, 'Prophesy to the breath, prophesy, son of man, and say to the breath of life ... "breathe on these slain, that they may live."' Then the breath of life, or the Spirit of God, came on those corpses, transforming them into a mighty, living army.

Ezekiel 37 is referring to the nation of Israel, with a prophecy about the unfolding drama of the nation. But there is a pattern here: the word of God (which Ezekiel preached) plus the Spirit of God (the breath of life) bring about new life or new birth. The challenge of this passage is to pray as well as to proclaim. Maybe our sowing of the gospel seed is becoming scarce and less fruitful because our prayer meetings have diminished or disappeared. We are to speak of Jesus to society in the power of the Holy Spirit. This will be effective if our walk and witness is covered with much prayer, both individually and corporately.

As we proclaim God's word, God by His Holy Spirit takes hold of that word, applying it to the heart of the hearer, to bring about spiritual rebirth. Derek Bingham, a Northern Irish preacher, explained, 'Gentle words fall lightly, but they have great weight.' As I preach or witness, or simply give away a tract, I pray that the Lord will use the gospel to save people. We scatter the gospel seed and wait for God to do His work as it is planted in good soil.

Lord, lay some soul upon my heart,
And love that soul through me;
That I may nobly do my part
To win that soul for Thee.[2]

We scatter seed where we can, but it is surely right to be intentional about sowing seed in prepared soil. I have a burden for the children and grandchildren of Christians because a huge number are turning their back on the Lord. I therefore believe in the value of making a date to meet up with children or grandchildren, perhaps treating them to a lovely meal, but aiming specifically to talk them through the gospel and lovingly challenge them to trust Jesus as their Lord and Saviour. It should be an occasion which has been saturated with prayer, and God can do His work. I can picture my grandmother talking my older brother through *The Wordless Book* when he was fourteen years old. It was a sacred moment that has stayed with me.[3]

John Watson, a Scottish theologian (1850–1907), wrote to fellow preachers, 'Be kind, you do not know what battles people are fighting.' People bear a variety of disappointed dreams, shattered hopes, fears, even terrors. It is to such people that we are speaking of Jesus, the friend of sinners.

Whilst I was speaking at a Young Life Sports Camp, a teenager who had tears in his eyes approached me: 'Roger eleven years ago you buried my father.' He told me more before saying, 'I miss him so much, but I don't remember him.' I was able to tell him what a wonderful Christian his father had been, and how pleased he would have been to know that his son was on the camp. My point is that before he spoke to me, I was unaware that this teenager was on that camp. We often do not know to whom we are speaking, but each will have their needs.

Conscience is the evangelist's ally. Whilst we speak and the Holy Spirit is working, the individual's conscience may well be accusing the listener. People know that they are not the people they want to be or should be. A hospital chaplain, whilst doing his rounds, regularly asked one patient, 'Is there anything I can do for you?' The repeated reply was a definite 'No!' until one day the bed-ridden gentleman replied, 'No, but I wish there were some things you could undo for me!' No one, outside of Jesus, can deal with the two problems which every individual faces: those of sin and death. Only Jesus can forgive sin and defeat death.

Many of the people to whom we witness will put on a mask of indifference, but we never know what is churning in their minds. Whilst we seek to live a consistent Christian life – quietly but faithfully praying, and taking the opportunities to speak – there may be a new openness to the gospel in time. When I was first converted, I witnessed to my father's secretary of twenty-five years. She verbally put me down and I parted with my tail between my legs! But nearly twenty years later, I bumped into her on our town's main street. As we began talking, she told me that her youngest son had become a born-again Christian. When I asked her if she too had been born again, she replied, 'No ... but I would love to be!' The next day, I had the privilege of leading her to Christ. She went on to become strong in her faith. My timing for her conversion was not the same as God's, but He was at work all along. God has promised, 'So shall My word be that goes forth from My mouth; it shall not return to Me void, but it shall accomplish what I please, and it shall prosper in the thing for which I sent it' (Isaiah 55:11). Some seed will fall on good ground and will yield a crop – 'some a hundredfold, some sixty, some thirty' (Matthew 13:8). We can pray to that end. Let us earnestly pray that God would use us to become soul-winners.

Whilst we will want to share the gospel as lovingly as we can, there has to be some thickness of skin because there are many who will reject what we say. John Wesley had dead cats thrown at him. In many parts of the world, Christians are persecuted in a way we in the West have not experienced for centuries. But indifference can be hurtful too. Like most of Charles Dickens' works, *The Pickwick Papers* was published in serial form and eagerly awaited by all. A clergyman at that time spent some time giving spiritual comfort to a sick parishioner. When he got up to leave, feeling that he had perhaps done some good, he heard the invalid mutter, 'Well, thank God *Pickwick* will be out in ten days anyway!' Sadly, some of the sown seed will fall on hard, stony or thorny ground. However, when there is rejection, we continue to sow, not knowing which seed will prosper.

Jesus said to His followers:

If the world hates you, you know that it hated Me before it hated you. If you were of the world, the world would love its own. Yet because you are not of the world, but I chose you out of the world, therefore the world hates you. Remember the word that I said to you, 'A servant is not greater than his master.' If they persecuted Me, they will also persecute you.

(John 15:18–20)

It is an easy error to conform our beliefs to current politically correct opinions, but it leads to insipid religion. We are not to be bombastic, but winsome; yet we are also to be faithful and true to Scripture.

The people we are reaching are not our enemies, even if they are the enemies of God. They are as we once were, and our prayer is that they will be as we are now. Towards the end of his short life, the American pastor Edward Payson wrote in 1827, 'I was never fit to speak a word to a sinner except when I had a broken heart myself … and felt as if I had just received pardon to my own soul – no anger, no anger.' Everyone we meet is made in the image of God; they are broken, but loved by God. That person may be broken in a different way to me, but my need was the same as their need is. There is no place for Phariseeism in a soul-winner's life. We have no right to look down on anyone, no matter how much they have scarred themselves in their fight against the Lord.

Our aim is not to win an argument, but to see people coming to saving faith in Christ. Actually, there are occasions when we might imagine there is going to be vibrant discussion, but instead there is a spiritual hunger which overrides natural antagonism. I was once travelling back home very late one Sunday night after preaching in Hastings. My dashboard was indicating that I was running out of fuel, but I was reluctant to buy petrol on a Sunday as I like to keep that day separate from any business transactions. However, necessity pressurised me. I filled up the tank, then went into the kiosk to pay. There was no one else queuing so I began chatting, asking the cashier if he was on duty all night. He replied, 'Yes, I'm on a fifteen-hour shift.'

'Oh dear', I responded. 'I suppose that means that you weren't able to go to church today?'

'Well, I am a Hindu,' he said.

To which I simply said, 'Oh that doesn't matter, everyone is welcome to church.'

This was the beginning of a forty-five minute conversation about the Lord. In fact, it was the first of many conversations I had with that young man. Regularly, I would go to the same garage late at night so that we could look at the Bible together. Whether he ever trusted the Lord, I don't know – on one visit I discovered he was not there; on enquiring I found he had moved on. He had always had a simple desire to know and understand more about the Lord, and now I pursue him with my prayers, so watering the sown seed.

4

We need to know when it is time to harvest and hoard the seed

One of the dangers in modern evangelism is that it lays the emphasis on decision for Christ instead of on surrender to Jesus Christ. That to me is a grave blunder. When a man decides for Christ he usually puts his confidence in his own honour, not in Christ at all.

Oswald Chambers[1]

We need wisdom to know when to 'put in the sickle', as Mark 4:29 instructs us, and harvest the spiritual crop which has now grown. As I have mentioned before, I have known individuals who always claimed to have led numerous people to Christ. I often wonder what their mindset was because exaggeration is dishonest and therefore sin. It is very exciting to see people coming to faith in Christ, and there should always be a sense of expectation that today could be a day when we are privileged to lead someone to Christ. However, we evangelise because we are under orders to do so, and not to chalk up successes. The greatest thing in life is to bring others to Jesus. David Brainerd, missionary to the Native Americans, said, 'There was nothing of any importance to me but holiness of heart and life, and the conversion of the Indians to God.'

Missions can be very exciting work for both churches and inter-denominational groups, but we need to recall the parable of the sower: some of the seed will fall by the wayside, and some that looks to have borne fruit will be scorched by the sun or strangled by thorns. Initially, things looked so promising, but clearly there was not sufficient depth for roots to shoot to produce fruit. Of course, some seed will fall in good ground and be productive, but let us be careful not to pronounce people saved who have only been moved by what they have heard, or even manipulated into making a decision. Churches, ministries and individuals can be guilty of doing this, thus making unsubstantiated claims. The 'converts' are not seen again.

We share the gospel, then in prayer we leave the rest to God. A highwayman once stopped John Wesley and demanded his money or his life. Wesley, after giving him his money, said, 'Let me speak one word to you; the time may come when you will regret the course of life in which you are now engaged. Remember this, "The blood of Jesus Christ cleanseth from all sin."' No more was said, and they parted. Years later, as Wesley was leaving a church at which he had preached, a stranger introduced himself and asked Wesley if he remembered being waylaid at such a time. 'I was that man,' said the stranger, 'and that single verse you quoted on that occasion was the means of a total change in my life and habits ... I trust I am now a true Christian.'

Of course, we each want to be effective evangelists. We thank God too for those who have been greatly used in reaping a vast harvest. Their names are remembered, even revered. However, I have been encouraged on several occasions by comments I read in an old book about Ruth as she gleaned in the fields (Ruth 2:17). It made these quaint points about the gleaner:

- The gleaner has to keep her eyes open.
- The gleaner stoops for all she gleans.

- The gleaner knows that each little stalk helps to make a bundle.
- The gleaner is as careful to retain as she is to obtain.[2]

I am convinced that we can expect that the Lord will use us to win people for Christ. We shouldn't need to seek help from another Christian when someone we meet wants to put their trust in Jesus. Some people are converted the first time they hear the gospel; others experience a much longer struggle to receive Jesus as their Lord and Saviour. Whatever the timing, we should be prepared to sit down with someone, explain the way of salvation and pray as they put their faith in Christ. When Paul and Silas were in prison in Philippi, and as an earthquake struck, the jailer asked them in desperation, 'Sirs, what must I do to be saved?' (Acts 16:30). They knew exactly what to say: 'Believe on the Lord Jesus Christ, and you will be saved ...' (Acts 16:31). They then led him and his family to Christ.

Each year, I like to have a motto. Last year, it was: 'A sower went forth to sow'. This year, I am using these words of Jesus: 'Follow Me, and I will make you fishers of men' (Matthew 4:19). I want not just to influence fish, but to catch them.

Lead me to some soul today,
O teach me, Lord, just what to say;
Friends of mine are lost in sin
And cannot find the way.
Few there are who seem to care
And few there are who pray;
Melt my heart and fill my life
Give me one soul today.[3]

If we are praying like this, the Lord may surprise us by giving us the privilege of leading someone to Christ. However, sometimes that means we have to put to death the plans we had made. For example, I recall travelling by train for a weekend of open-air preaching with United Beach Missions in Hyde Park Corner, London. On the journey I was under pressure to prepare sixteen evangelistic talks on John's Gospel for another mission. I sat in the very last carriage of the train, so as to be away from any distracting conversation. The carriage was empty … until we stopped at Wakefield. Suddenly, my carriage filled up. I put my head down, studying for my sermons on John's Gospel. A lady sat next to me. I thought I should begin a conversation with her, but felt I had to prepare the talks. And as she was a woman, I felt I couldn't speak to her!

My conscience pricked me, so I prayed, 'Lord, if you really want me to chat with her, may she start the conversation … but I would rather not. I have so much to do!' Almost before I had finished uttering 'Amen', the lady asked me why I was studying the Gospel of John. Aagh!

She told me that she had been divorced five days earlier. She was so upset she had gone to Wakefield Cathedral to ask to talk with someone, but no one was available. All week she had been in turmoil. It was the beginning of a conversation that ended when the train arrived at King's Cross station in London.

I passed on her information to a church in the village near Wakefield where she lived, and soon after she was converted. I suspect the Lord was testing my availability. When harvest time comes, the sickle needs to be put in, for the harvest is ready to reap or to rot.

If we are walking with the Lord, there should be a spirit of expectancy. The Lord will open doors of opportunity that we need to be willing to walk through and take. Sometimes, we have to go over to the doors and force them open, but there are moments that with winsome boldness we can take. If at present there appears to be great hardness of heart and spiritual apathy in someone, even antagonism, let us remind ourselves God takes 'no pleasure in the death of the wicked', but wants all men to be saved (Ezekiel 33:11; see also Matthew 23:37–39 and 1 Timothy 2:4).

The biblical principle is that where sin abounds, grace abounds much more. Often, throughout history, this has proved to be true not only for individuals, but in nations also. For example, when the Syrians misrepresented God, thus blaspheming Him, God ensured they were defeated in battle so that they would 'know that I am the LORD' (1 Kings 20:28). People will only be allowed to go so far before God either saves or judges, which is an encouragement for us to be urgently about our Father's business. We must remember that 'the LORD's hand is not shortened, that it cannot save' (Isaiah 59:1).

In spiritual harvesting, it is very helpful to take people to hear the public preaching of the gospel. Evangelistic services are such a blessing because they give us opportunity to bring friends and contacts to hear a clear, full presentation of Jesus' story. If there is an evangelistic mission being held anywhere near you, arrange for a group to go, and who knows what might happen.

Clergy and those in full-time ministry play a key role in modelling and energising an evangelistic emphasis in churches. However, there is a danger that those whose ministry is to lead a church lose the fire of evangelistic burden. A century ago, C.I. Scofield was a well-known pastor in Dallas, USA. Known for his strongly dispensational views, he was the original editor of *The Scofield Bible*. In 1918, he suffered a serious illness during which he was able to assess and evaluate his ministry. In January 1919, he wrote the following letter to many of his Bible teaching friends:

Dear and Honoured Brother,

You and I are Bible teachers. It is of God's grace and it is a great gift. But near to it is a great danger.

For many months I have, through physical disability, been laid aside from all oral ministry. During this time, it has been increasingly laid upon me that I should beg the forbearance of my teaching brethren whilst I state in plain truth the teacher's danger.

In a word, it is the neglect of the gospel message to the unsaved. But brother that is the great message. It is sweet and needful to feed the flock of Christ, but it is to seek and save lost men and women that Jesus came, died, and rose again. It is not enough to repeat gospel texts and say, 'Come to Jesus.' There is a tender seeking in the gospel truly preached.

How many gospel sermons did you preach in 1918? How many found salvation under your ministry? Let us make 1919 a mighty, tireless effort to save lost men.

Yours in Christ's love,

C.I. Scofield

There have been times when, with friends, I have put on an evangelistic event and brought together family, friends, neighbours and contacts. When I left school, I invited all my school friends and teachers to a lavish barbecue in my parents' garden, and asked my spiritual mentor, Prof. Verna Wright, to preach the gospel. I insisted that at my wedding service the gospel was to be preached. (Ministers can speak to the bride and groom at another time, but they will never have another opportunity to preach to the couple's family and friends as they do at their wedding service.) We had the gospel proclaimed at the thanksgiving services of each of our four children. On certain 'big birthdays' I have arranged an evangelistic birthday event, with food, music and a gospel presentation. We have done similarly on special wedding anniversaries. They have all proved to be valuable times, and because of the occasion, there has consistently been a positive response to the message. Each guest is given a carefully wrapped evangelistic book. Of course, Christmas is another special occasion, so to have a guest event with a Christmas theme is always appreciated. Why don't you work with others from your church to arrange an evangelistic event for a special occasion? They provide an opportunity to reap, which is not always easy with those who have become friends.

Psalm 126:5–6 has heart-warming words for every soul-winner: 'Those who sow in tears shall reap in joy. He who continually goes forth weeping, bearing seed for sowing, shall doubtless come again with rejoicing, bringing his sheaves with him.' However, in the preceding verses, the psalmist is recalling times of great blessing, when there was joy, laughter and rejoicing. Now things had become arid and barren. There was little evidence of God working. In verse 4, he prays to God, before encouraging himself with the truths of the last two verses. No matter how tough our evangelism work may appear to be, let us claim the promises of God:

For as the rain comes down and the snow from heaven,
And do not return there,
But water the earth,
And make it bring forth and bud,

We need to know when it is time to harvest and hoard the seed

That it may give seed to the sower
And bread to the eater,
So shall My word be that goes forth from My mouth;
It shall not return to Me void,
But it shall accomplish what I please,
And it shall prosper in the thing for which I sent it.
(Isaiah 55:10–11)

We are to go into the harvest field of the world for the glory of God, sharing the gospel, the only way of salvation, with all people we can.

Dawson Trotman, the founder of The Navigators, was a soul-winner and a disciple-maker, whose influence spread through the world. Ministering in Schroon Lake in Upstate New York, he and Jack Wyrtzen took two teenagers on the lake in a motorboat. But in turning the boat at speed, both young people were thrown out of the boat into the water. They both cried out, 'I can't swim!' Trotman dived in to rescue them. He got the first and then the other near the boat, and Wyrtzen pulled each to safety. As Trotman put out his hand to be pulled up, somehow Wyrtzen's grip slipped, and Trotman went under. Wyrtzen later said, 'The whole of the US Navy could not have saved Dawson: his time was up!' *Time* magazine carried his obituary, and under Trotman's photograph were the words: 'Always holding somebody up'. Isn't that our calling today? Nothing lifts a person like the gospel; there is no Saviour other than Jesus, and no different way of salvation than through His forgiveness and new life.

The Lord has entrusted to us the most valuable service of proclaiming Christ to a lost world, which is without hope because it is without Christ. I pray that we will be obedient to this heavenly calling to make Christ known, and then to make disciples of those who repent and believe. Napoleon Bonaparte's lieutenants carried in their jackets, therefore close to their hearts, a map of the world because it was Napoleon's purpose to conquer the world, and so their goal too. For that vain aim they sacrificed, fought, suffered and died. Ours is a much more glorious cause, and we know that one day every knee will bow to King Jesus. There is such joy in living and witnessing for Jesus. What would hold us back from such an honoured calling?

A favourite Bible verse of mine is: 'In the morning sow your seed, and in the evening do not withhold your hand; for you do not know which will prosper, either this or that, or whether both alike will be good' (Ecclesiastes 11:6).

Dear Lord, I ask for the eyes that see
Deep down to the world's sore need;
I ask for a love that holds not back,
But pours out itself in deed.
I want the passionate power of prayer
That yearns for the great crowd's soul;
I want to go 'mongst the fainting sheep
And tell them my Lord makes whole.[4]

Recommended reading on the theme of soul-winning

What a privilege is ours to have such a vast array of Christian books. This may not be the case forever (Elton John has called for religion to be banned completely), and we know that when books are burned, very soon after people are too.[1] But at present, if we turn away from laziness and the lure of television, all of us have time to soak up the finest of people's study and experience. This will fill our minds with treasures that expand them and enrich our lives.

One of the many attributes of my wife is that she has never grumbled when I have come home with yet another book. Together we have enjoyed nosing along our book shelves to extract a volume which becomes part of our conversation, influencing our thinking and perhaps even our lives. But I don't keep books for the sake of it; they are tools that I want to use. Frankly, if after a few chapters I am not gleaning what I want, I move on. As the Italians say, 'There is no worse thief than a bad book!'

I have found books to be the most delightful companions. They are not flesh and blood yet they speak and stimulate, and have proved to be faithful and proficient teachers. They have entertained me when I have needed fun (I have all the annuals of the cartoonist Matt); they have shown me the way when I have needed instruction; they have fed my mind when it felt starved; and they have travelled with me when I have been alone.

With a few exceptions, I am too utilitarian – and too slow a reader – to enjoy novels. However, I have found that good Christian biography sharpens me up spiritually and fuels the imagination as much as fiction would. I love missionary biographies from the nineteenth and twentieth centuries. Many are out of print, but can be found in good Christian second-hand bookshops. C.S. Lewis advocated reading every good book at least once every ten years, and stated that the more up-to-date a book was, the sooner it would become dated. King Solomon famously said, 'Of making many books there is no end, and much study is wearisome to the flesh' (Ecclesiastes 12:12).

Nevertheless, below is a list of books which I have found to be of great help to me in the work of soul-winning. I wholeheartedly commend them to you.

Eighteenth-Century Christian Leaders by J.C. Ryle (first published 1869; new edition: Evangelical Press, 2018).

The Cross of Christ by John Stott (first published 1986; twentieth anniversary edition: IVP, 2006).

Daws by Betty Skinner (NavPress, 1998).

The Evangelism Mandate by David Larsen (Kregel Publications, 2002).

Evangelistic Preaching by Roger Carswell (10Publishing, 2015).

Facing a Task Unfinished by Roger Carswell (Christian Focus Publications, 2015).

Five English Reformers by J.C. Ryle (Banner of Truth, 1960).

George Whitefield by Arnold Dallimore (Banner of Truth, 1970).

Living Faith by Helen Roseveare (first published 1980; new edition: Christian Focus Publications, 2007).

Living Sacrifice by Helen Roseveare (Christian Focus Publications, 2007).

Listening to the Giants by Warren Wiersbe (Baker, 1979).

J. Hudson Taylor: A Man in Christ by Roger Steer (first published 1990; new edition: Authentic Media, 2001).

Milestones of the Master by Warren Wiersbe (Weaver Book Company, 2015).

Ministering like the Master by Stuart Olyott (Banner of Truth, 2017).

Moody by John Pollock (first published 1983; new edition: Christian Focus Publications, 2005).

A Prophet with Honor: The Billy Graham Story by Walter Martin (updated edition: Zondervan, 2018).

Richard Hobson of Liverpool by Richard Hobson (new edition: Banner of Truth, 2003).

Sacrifice by Simon Guillebaud (10Publishing, 2013).

True Discipleship by William MacDonald (revised and updated edition: Gospel Folio Press, 2016).

Walking with the Giants by Warren Wiersbe (Baker, 1976).

Wesley's Journal, an abridged edition (various editions are available).

10ofthose.com sell numerous books, booklets and tracts for evangelistic work, and are always ready to advise as to the best for your purposes.

Notes

Introduction

1. Frances E. Scott, *Dare and Persevere: The Story of One Hundred Years of Evangelism in Syria and Lebanon from 1860 to 1960* (Lebanon Evangelical Mission, 1960).

2. The hymn 'Let me look at the crowd as my Saviour did', written by R.A. Jarvie.

1. We need to ensure that we get the right seed

1. Leighton Ford, *The Christian Persuader: The Urgency of Evangelism in Today's World* (first published 1966; new edition: Rosarium Publishing, 2017).

2. For resurrection to be preached, crucifixion must have first been proclaimed. So Paul's dictum, 'I determined not to know anything among you except Jesus Christ and Him crucified' (1 Corinthians 2:2), is consistent with the sermon-summaries we read in Acts. 2.

2. We need to sow and scatter the seed

1. Handel's *Messiah* (1741), based on Psalm 68:11.

2. Clarence W. Hall, *Samuel Logan Brengle: Portrait of a Prophet* (originally published 1929).

3. The particular wallet I use appears to be purpose-made for the size and shape of tracts published by 10Publishing.

4. The hymn 'There's a work for Jesus', written by Elsie Duncan Yale (1912).

5. G.N.M. Collins, *Men of the Burning Heart* (Knox Press, 1983).

6. *Richard Hobson of Liverpool: The Autobiography of a Faithful Pastor* (new edition: Banner of Truth, 2003).

7. Frances E. Scott, *Dare and Persevere*.

3. We need to wait and water the seed

1. Warren W. Wiersbe, *His Name Is Wonderful* (Tyndale House, 1976).

2. The anonymous hymn 'Lord, lay some soul upon my heart'.

3. *The Wordless Book* is an evangelistic booklet designed to explain the gospel for children.

4. We need to know when it is time to harvest and hoard the seed

1. Oswald Chambers, *Shade of His Hand* (first published 1924; new edition: Discovery House Publishers, 1989).

2. This book was *Biblical Encyclopaedia and Museum*, Volume 3, by James Cowper Gray.

3. The hymn 'Lead me to some soul today', written by Will Henry Houghton.

4. The largely forgotten hymn 'With a soul blood bought, and a heart aglow'.

Recommend reading on the theme of soul-winning

1. The Observer newspaper's *Monthly Music Magazine* (12 November 2006).

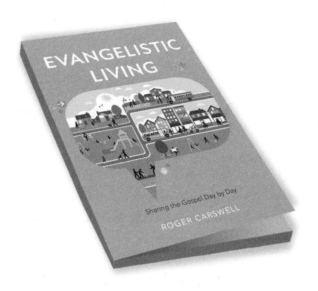

EVANGELISTIC LIVING

Sharing the Gospel Day by Day

ROGER CARSWELL

10 Publishing
a division of 10ofthose.com

10Publishing is the publishing house of 10ofThose.
It is committed to producing quality Christian
resources that are biblical and accessible.

www.10ofthose.com is our online retail arm selling
thousands of quality books at discounted prices.

For information contact: info@10ofthose.com
or check out our website: www.10ofthose.com